interchange

FIFTH EDITION

T0343951

3B

Workbook

Jack C. Richards

with Jonathan Hull and Susan Proctor

CAMBRIDGE
UNIVERSITY PRESS

University Printing House, Cambridge CB2 8BS, United Kingdom

One Liberty Plaza, 20th Floor, New York, NY 10006, USA

477 Williamstown Road, Port Melbourne, VIC 3207, Australia

4843/24, 2nd Floor, Ansari Road, Daryaganj, Delhi – 110002, India

79 Anson Road, #06–04/06, Singapore 079906

Cambridge University Press is part of the University of Cambridge.

It furthers the University's mission by disseminating knowledge in the pursuit of education, learning and research at the highest international levels of excellence.

www.cambridge.org
Information on this title: www.cambridge.org/9781316622797

First published 1991
Second edition 1998
Third edition 2005
Fourth edition 2013
20 19 18 17 16 15 14 13 12 11 10 9 8 7 6 5 4 3 2 1

Printed in Malaysia by Vivar Printing

A catalogue record for this publication is available from the British Library.

ISBN	9781316620519	Student's Book with Online Self-Study 3
ISBN	9781316620533	Student's Book with Online Self-Study 3A
ISBN	9781316620540	Student's Book with Online Self-Study 3B
ISBN	9781316620557	Student's Book with Online Self-Study and Online Workbook 3
ISBN	9781316620564	Student's Book with Online Self-Study and Online Workbook 3A
ISBN	9781316620588	Student's Book with Online Self-Study and Online Workbook 3B
ISBN	9781316622766	Workbook 3
ISBN	9781316622773	Workbook 3A
ISBN	9781316622797	Workbook 3B
ISBN	9781316622803	Teacher's Edition with Complete Assessment Program 3
ISBN	9781316622308	Class Audio CDs 3
ISBN	9781316624050	Full Contact with Online Self-Study 3
ISBN	9781316624074	Full Contact with Online Self-Study 3A
ISBN	9781316624098	Full Contact with Online Self-Study 3B
ISBN	9781316622322	Presentation Plus 3

Additional resources for this publication at www.cambridge.org/interchange

Contents

Credits

The authors and publishers acknowledge the following sources of copyright material and are grateful for the permissions granted. While every effort has been made, it has not always been possible to identify the sources of all the material used, or to trace all copyright holders. If any omissions are brought to our notice, we will be happy to include the appropriate acknowledgements on reprinting and in the next update to the digital edition, as applicable.

Key: BL = Below Left, BR = Below Right, C = Centre, CL = Centre Left, CR = Centre Right, TC = Top Centre, TL = Top Left, TR = Top Right.

Illustrations

337 Jon (KJA Artists): 51; **Mark Duffin**: 31, 80; **Pablo Gallego** (Beehive Illustration): 10, 20; **Thomas Girard** (Good Illustration): 4, 28, 53; **Dusan Lakicevic** (Beehive Illustration): 1, 14, 22, 33, 96; **Yishan Li** (Advocate Art): 6, 13, 65; **Quino Marin** (The Organisation): 29; **Gavin Reece** (New Division): 3, 64; **Paul Williams** (Sylvie Poggio Artists): 15, 66.

Photos

Back cover (woman with whiteboard): Jenny Acheson/Stockbyte/GettyImages; Back cover (whiteboard): Nemida/GettyImages; Back cover (man using phone): Betsie Van Der Meer/Taxi/GettyImages; Back cover (woman smiling): PeopleImages.com/DigitalVision/GettyImages; Back cover (name tag): Tetra Images/GettyImages; Back cover (handshake): David Lees/Taxi/GettyImages; p. 2 : Michael H/DigitalVision/GettyImages; p. 5 (TL): Jade/Blend Images/Getty Images Plus/GettyImages; p. 5 (TR): Jamie Grill/GettyImages; p. 5 (BL): Blend Images - Jose Luis Pelaez Inc/Brand X Pictures/GettyImages; p. 5 (BR): Tomasz Trojanowski/Hemera/Getty Images Plus/GettyImages; p. 7: John Rowley/Photodisc/GettyImages; p. 8: KidStock/Blend Images/GettyImages; p. 9: monkeybusinessimages/iStock/Getty Images Plus/GettyImages; p. 12 (TL): ColorBlind/The Image Bank/GettyImages; p. 12 (TR): Sigrid Gombert/MITO images/GettyImages; p. 12 (CL): 4x6/E+/GettyImages; p. 12 (CR): Roy Hsu/Photographer's Choice RF/GettyImages; p. 13 (TR): mediaphotos/iStock/Getty Images Plus/GettyImages; p. 16: Purestock/GettyImages; p. 17 : PeopleImages/DigitalVision/GettyImages; p. 18: Phil Boorman/Cultura/GettyImages; p. 19 (TL): Robert George Young/Photographer's Choice/GettyImages; p. 19 (BR): dangdumrong/iStock/Getty Images Plus/GettyImages; p. 21 (TR): Chris Dyball/Innerlight/The Image Bank/GettyImages; p. 21 (CL): MattStansfield/iStock/Getty Images Plus/GettyImages; p. 23: EXTREME-PHOTOGRAPHER/E+/GettyImages; p. 24 (Johnson): George Doyle/Stockbyte/GettyImages; p. 24 (Marshall): Digital Vision./Photodisc/GettyImages; p. 24 (James): Yellow Dog Productions/The Image Bank/GettyImages; p. 24 (Grant): wdstock/iStock/Getty Images Plus/GettyImages; p. 24 (Simpson): Dave and Les Jacobs/Blend Images/GettyImages; p. 25 (TR): asiseeit/iStock/Getty Images Plus/GettyImages; p. 25 (BR): hadynyah/E+/GettyImages; p. 26: Thomas_EyeDesign/Vetta/GettyImages; p. 30: Education Images/Universal Images Group/GettyImages; p. 32 (George): snapphoto/E+/GettyImages; p. 32 (airport): Philippe TURPIN/Photononstop/Photolibrary/GettyImages; p. 32 (Diane): Vesnaandjic/E+/GettyImages; p. 32 (car): lisegagne/E+/GettyImages; p. 34: Whiteway/E+/GettyImages; p. 35 (wrench): TokenPhoto/E+/GettyImages; p. 35 (TR): John E. Kelly/Photodisc/GettyImages; p. 36: pixelfusion3d/iStock/Getty Images Plus/GettyImages; p. 37 (drain): belovodchenko/iStock/Getty Images Plus/GettyImages; p. 37 (plane): incposterco/E+/GettyImages; p. 37 (smoke): Harrison Shull/Aurora/GettyImages; p. 37 (land): Sierralara/RooM/GettyImages; p. 38 (forest): Ro-Ma Stock Photography/Photolibrary/GettyImages; p. 39: Howard Shooter/Dorling Kindersley/GettyImages; p. 40: VCG/Contributor/Visual China Group/GettyImages; p. 41: Travel Ink/Gallo Images/The Image Bank/GettyImages; p. 42: SolStock/iStock/Getty Images Plus/GettyImages; p. 43: Doug Armand/Oxford Scientific/GettyImages; p. 44: Wilfried Krecichwost/DigitalVision/GettyImages; p. 45: cglade/E+/GettyImages; p. 46 (TL): Lew Robertson/StockFood Creative/GettyImages; p. 46 (TC): Alina555/iStock/Getty Images Plus/GettyImages; p. 46 (TR): Jose Luis Pelaez Inc/Blend Images/GettyImages; p. 47 (photo 1): Hemera Technologies/PhotoObjects.net/Getty Images Plus/GettyImages; p. 47 (photo 2): Picturenet/Blend Images/GettyImages; p. 47 (photo 3): Zoran Milich/Photodisc/GettyImages; p.47 (photo 4): DragonImages/iStock/Getty Images Plus/GettyImages; p. 48 (TR): BrianAJackson/iStock/Getty Images Plus/GettyImages; p. 48 (CR): reka prod./Westend61/GettyImages; p. 49 (TR): simazoran/iStock/Getty Images Plus/Getty Image; p. 49 (CR): ONOKY - Eric Audras/Brand X Pictures/GettyImages; p. 49 (BR): michaeljung/iStock/Getty Images Plus/GettyImages; p. 50: leaf/iStock/Getty Images Plus/GettyImages; p. 52 (TL): IP Galanternik D.U./E+/GettyImages; p. 52 (TR): Lady-Photo/iStock/Getty Images Plus/GettyImages; p. 54: Westend61/GettyImages; p. 55 (CR): Andy Sheppard/Redferns/GettyImages; p. 55 (BR): by Roberto Peradotto/Moment/GettyImages; p. 56 (L): Mint/Hindustan Times/GettyImages; p. 56 (R): Michael Runkel/imageBROKER/GettyImages; p. 57: Bettmann/GettyImages; p. 58 (TL): Bettmann/GettyImages; p. 58 (BR): Ron Levine/Photographer's Choice/GettyImages; p. 59: Windsor & Wiehahn/Stone/GettyImages; p. 60: Javier Pierini/Stone/GettyImages; p. 61: blackred/iStock/Getty Images Plus/GettyImages; p. 62: izusek/iStock/Getty Images Plus/GettyImages; p. 63: ADRIAN DENNIS/AFP/GettyImages; p. 67: Greg Vaughn/Perspectives/GettyImages; p. 68: Caiaimage/Robert Daly/GettyImages; p. 69 (TL): marco wong/Moment/GettyImages; p. 69 (TR): Oscar Wong/Moment Open/GettyImages; p. 69 (CL): Otto Stadler/Photographer's Choice/GettyImages; p. 69 (CR): David Hannah/Lonely Planet Images/GettyImages; p. 69 (BL): LOOK Photography/UpperCut Images/GettyImages; p. 69 (BR): lightkey/E+/GettyImages; p. 70: Thomas Kokta/Photographer's Choice RF/GettyImages; p. 71 (Calgary Farmers' Market): Ken Woo/Calgary Farmers' Market; p. 71 (WWF): © naturepl.com/Andy Rouse/WWF; p. 72: Christian Hoehn/Taxi/GettyImages; p. 73 (TL): Rosanna U/Image Source/GettyImages; p. 73 (TC): Mark Weiss/Photodisc/GettyImages; p. 73 (TR): i love images/Cultura/GettyImages; p. 73 (BL): monkeybusinessimages/iStock/Getty Images Plus/GettyImages; p. 73 (BC): Photo and Co/The Image Bank/GettyImages; p. 73 (BR): Alija/E+/GettyImages; p. 74 (stonehenge): Maxine Bolton/EyeEm/GettyImages; p. 74 (people): Peter Dennis/GettyImages; p. 74 (boats): De Agostini/M. Seemuller/De Agostini Picture Library/GettyImages; p. 75 (bigfoot): Big_Ryan/DigitalVision Vectors/GettyImages; p. 75 (footprints): Danita Delimont/Gallo Images/GettyImages; p. 76: Steve Bronstein/Stone/GettyImages; p. 77: kbeis/DigitalVision Vectors/GettyImages; p. 78: mediaphotos/Vetta/GettyImages; p. 79 (T): Oscar Garces/CON/LatinContent Editorial/GettyImages; p. 81: Theo Wargo/Getty Images North America/GettyImages; p. 82 (TL): ColorBlind Images/Blend Images/GettyImages; p. 82 (TR): track5/E+/GettyImages; p. 83: imagenavi/GettyImages; p. 84 (TL): John Wildgoose/GettyImages; p. 84 (TR): Bloomberg/GettyImages; p. 84 (CL): Chris Ryan/Caiaimage/GettyImages; p. 84 (CR): numbeos/E+/GettyImages; p. 84 (BL): Tom Merton/OJO Images/GettyImages; p. 84 (BR): Ariel Skelley/Blend Images/GettyImages; p. 85 (TL): marcoventuriniautieri/E+/GettyImages; p. 85 (TR): Anadolu Agency/GettyImages; p. 85 (CL): Caspar Benson/GettyImages; p. 85 (CR): Jake Olson Studios Blair Nebraska/Moment/GettyImages; p. 86 (house): Peter Baker/GettyImages; p. 86 (traffic): Levi Bianco/Moment/GettyImages; p. 86 (bike): Billy Hustace/The Image Bank/GettyImages; p. 86 (using mobile): SolStock/E+/GettyImages; p. 87: Image Source/DigitalVision/GettyImages; p. 89: Caiaimage/Paul Bradbury/Riser/GettyImages; p. 90: Dawid Garwol/EyeEm/GettyImages; p. 92: FatCamera/E+/GettyImages; p. 93: c.Zeitgeist/Everett/REX/Shutterstock; p. 94 (TR): shapecharge/E+/GettyImages; p. 94 (BR): borgogniels/iStock/Getty Images Plus/GettyImages; p. 95: Lucidio Studio, Inc./Moment/GettyImages.

Getting things done

1 Which service does each person need? Choose the correct word or phrase.

- ☐ computer repair
- ☐ dry cleaning
- ☐ home repairs
- ☐ house painting
- ☐ language tutoring
- ☑ lawn mowing

1. _____ lawn mowing _____

Ken: I have a new home and don't have much time for yard work. I mowed the lawn two weeks ago, and I need to cut it again. I'd like to save money, but perhaps I'll just have to pay someone to do it for me.

2. _____

Akiko: I don't like the flowered wallpaper in my bedroom or the dark color of the walls in my living room. I want to have the wallpaper removed so the whole place looks bigger and brighter with fun, modern colors everywhere.

3. _____

Margaret: Now that it's getting colder, I need to take my winter clothes out of storage. Some things I can wash in the washing machine, but I should take my wool coat to that new place around the corner.

4. _____

Steven: I have a lot of work to do this week, but my laptop stopped working! I tried to fix it, but I don't know how. I can't afford to buy a new laptop.

5. _____

Eric: I'm so excited! I'm finally going to Quebec this summer. I studied French in high school, but I'm not sure how much I remember now. Do you know anyone who can help me improve my French?

6. _____

Karen: I really want to move into that studio apartment I found downtown. The only problem is that there are a lot of little things that need to be repaired. Where can I get a leaky faucet and a broken lock repaired?

home repairs

language tutoring

lawn mowing

2 Where can I get . . . ?

A Match the verbs in column A with the nouns in column B.

A	B	
cut	a stain	1. ___cut my hair___
check	my blood pressure	2. _____
do	my computer	3. _____
fix	my hair	4. _____
print	my nails	5. _____
remove	my pants	6. _____
shorten	my photos	7. _____

B First, use the items in part A to write *Where can I get . . . ?* or *Where can I have . . . ?* questions for speaker A. Then write responses for speaker B using your own ideas.

1. **A:** _Where can I get my hair cut?_
   B: _You can get it cut at May's Salon._

2. **A:** _____
   _____
   B: _____
   _____

3. **A:** _____
   _____
   B: _____
   _____

4. **A:** _____
   _____
   B: _____
   _____

5. **A:** _____
   _____
   B: _____
   _____

6. **A:** _____
   _____
   B: _____
   _____

7. **A:** _____
   _____
   B: _____
   _____

3 **Where can you have these services done? Write sentences with *You can have . . . .***

Come to
SALON 21
for an
AMAZING
haircut!

1. <u>You can have your hair cut at Salon 21.</u>

At *KWIK FIX*
we repair all kinds
of shoes.

2. _____

**DREAM
CLEAN**

We dry-clean
your clothes
like no
one else.

3. _____

**CARPET
WORLD**

*We'll clean your
carpets so they're
as good as new.*

4. _____

We do nails (and only nails)
at Nail File.

5. _____

JIMMY'S...

*...the best
car wash in town!*

6. _____

*Service your
washing machine
to keep it running
its best.*
**Call Hal's Repairs
at 555-1838**

7. _____

At EYE to EYE,

we can examine your eyes
in 30 minutes.

8. _____

A Look at the two pictures. Where have you dreamed about living, in an apartment in the city or in a house in the suburbs? Why? Where would your parents like to live? Why?

DOWNSIZING

Do you want your parents' furniture, family photos, old toys, and sports equipment? If you're a millennial, the answer is likely to be "no."

Millennials are people who became adults at the beginning of the 21st century, and they are not necessarily interested in collecting things. And boomers, Americans born in the years after World War II, are finding out that their children have very different ideas about how to live "the good life."

Millennials do not feel the need to have a lot of *things*. They would rather have *experiences*, like tourism, art, and sports activities. This preference for "less is better" – or downsizing – is partly a result of the world economic crisis and the student debt that many young adults have. The lack of jobs has made millennials want to lower their expenses. And they feel that they must pay off their student loans before they can get married and have children of their own.

Because millennials are waiting to start families, they tend to prefer to live in apartments rather than large houses like their parents. First, they simply don't need that much space. Second, houses are expensive. Third, houses are often located in the suburbs, farther away from the culture and diversity that cities have to offer and that many millennials want.

But, in the latest twist of generational clashes, millennials are finding it more and more difficult to afford city living. Boomers, who generally have more money to spend than millennials, are finally ready to sell their houses now that their children have moved out. When they do, many then use that money to buy an apartment in the city where they can start a new life with all the amenities cities have to offer to people with money.

With this increase in demand, the prices of apartments have gone up, and millennials are discovering that it is very difficult to compete economically with their boomer parents. One option is for millennials to live together. Today some of them are renting houses or large apartments that several people can share. More than a few people think that this kind of downsizing, besides being good for the pocketbook, is good for the planet.

B Read the article about downsizing. Check (✓) the true statements. For statements that are false, write the true information.

1. ☐ Adult children still enjoy receiving furniture from their parents.

_____

2. ☐ Boomers are Americans born before World War II.

_____

3. ☐ Downsizing is the philosophy that "less is better."

_____

4. ☐ The competition between boomers and millennials has a lot to do with money.

_____

5. ☐ The next step in downsizing could be for boomers and millennials to share houses and large apartments.

_____

5 Write two suggestions for each of these problems.

1. **A:** I never have any energy, so I can never do anything except work. I sleep all weekend, so don't tell me to get more rest!

   B: Have you thought about *taking an aerobics class?*
   Another option is to improve your diet.

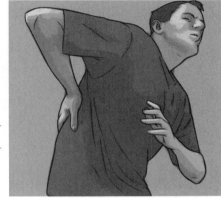

2. **A:** My problem is a constant backache. I just don't know what to do to get rid of it. I had someone give me a massage, but it didn't really help.

   B: Maybe you could _____

   _____

3. **A:** My doctor told me to get more exercise. She strongly recommended swimming, but I find swimming so boring! In fact, aren't all sports boring?

   B: Why don't you _____

   _____

4. **A:** I'm very sociable, and I have great difficulty saying no. I end up doing things every night of the week – going to parties, clubs, the movies. I'm so tired all the time!

   B: It might be a good idea _____

   _____

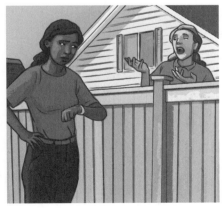

5. **A:** I like to be a good neighbor, but the woman next door drives me crazy. She's always knocking on my door to chat. And whenever I go out into the yard, she goes into her yard – and talks for hours!

   B: What about _____

   _____

6 Choose the correct three-word phrasal verb for each sentence.

1. I don't know how my grandmother _____ all the new technology. She's better at understanding new gadgets than I am! (comes up with / cuts down on / keeps up with)

2. My cousin didn't know what to do for her mother's 60th birthday, but she finally _____ the idea of a surprise picnic with the whole family. (came up with / got along with / looked forward to)

3. Ilene has done it again! She only met Chris two months ago, and already she has _____ him. Why doesn't she try to work out any problems? (broken up with / gotten along with / kept up with)

4. After Michelle saw her doctor, she decided to _____ eating fast food. She wants to lose some weight and start exercising again in order to keep fit. (cut down on / look forward to / take care of)

5. We're really lucky in my family because we all _____ each other very well. (come up with / get along with / look forward to)

6. I've done pretty badly in my classes this semester, so I'm not really _____ receiving my grades. (getting along with / looking forward to / taking care of)

7. I can't _____ that loud music anymore! I can't stand hip-hop, and I'm going to tell my neighbor right now. (cut down on / put up with / take care of)

8. I've been getting sick a lot lately, and I often feel tired. I really need to start _____ my health. (cutting down on / keeping up with / taking care of)

10 A matter of time

1 Circle the correct word that describes each sentence.

1. Events in December 2010 led to the peaceful removal of Tunisia's prime minister in January 2011. (natural disaster / epidemic / (revolution))

2. In 2014, a new species of insect was found in Vietnam. It has a body over 30 centimeters long and is the second longest insect in the world. (discovery / invention / epidemic)

3. On June 12, 2016, a gunman entered a nightclub in Florida where he killed 49 people and injured more than 50. (invention / terrorist act / achievement)

4. Advances in robot technology have come a long way in recent years. Scientists like Japan's Hiroshi Ishiguro have created human-like robots that can have conversations with each other and with humans. (achievement / disaster / terrorist act)

5. Prime Minister Benazir Bhutto of Pakistan was killed after leaving a campaign rally in December 2007. (assassination / election / revolution)

6. In 2010, a series of floods in Australia affected over 200,000 people and caused nearly a billion Australian dollars in damage. (discovery / natural disaster / epidemic)

2 Complete the sentences. Use words from the box.

ago	for	from	in	since	to

1. Jazz first became popular _____in_____ the 1920s.

2. The cell phone was invented about 45 years _____.

3. Brasília has been the capital city of Brazil _____ 1960.

4. The first laptop was produced _____ 1981.

5. Mexico has been independent _____ more than 200 years.

6. World War II lasted _____ 1939 _____ 1945.

7. Vietnam was separated into two parts _____ about 20 years.

8. East and West Germany have been united _____ 1990.

jazz

Brasília

3 Nouns and verbs

A Complete this chart. Then check your answers in a dictionary.

Noun	Verb	Noun	Verb
achievement	_achieve_	existence	_____
assassination	_____	exploration	_____
demonstration	_____	explosion	_____
discovery	_____	invention	_____
discrimination	_____	transformation	_____
election	_____	vaccination	_____

B Choose verbs from the chart in part A to complete these sentences. Use the correct verb tense.

Bangalore, a high-tech center

a research station in Antarctica

1. Over the past several decades, the Indian city of Bangalore has _transformed_ itself into a high-tech center.

2. In World War I, many soldiers were _____ against typhoid, a deadly bacterial disease.

3. Aung San, the man who led Myanmar to independence, was _____ in 1947. No one is certain who killed him.

4. The European Union has _____ since 1957.

5. Until the 1960s, there were many laws that _____ against African Americans in certain regions of the United States.

6. In 1885, Louis Pasteur _____ a cure for rabies when he treated a young boy who was bitten by a dog.

7. In recent years, teams of experts in countries such as Cambodia and Angola have been safely _____ land mines in order to rid those countries of these dangerous weapons.

8. One of the few parts of the world that has not been _____ much is Antarctica. The extreme climate makes it dangerous to travel far from research centers.

4 Vaccines past, present, and future

A What are vaccinations? If necessary, scan the article to find out.

VACCINATIONS

For well over a thousand years, smallpox was a disease that everyone feared. The disease killed much of the native population in South America when the Spanish arrived there in the early sixteenth century. By the end of the eighteenth century, smallpox was responsible for the deaths of about one in ten people around the world. Those who survived the disease were left with ugly scars on their skin.

It had long been well known among farmers that people who worked with cows rarely caught smallpox; instead, they often caught a similar but much milder disease called cowpox. A British doctor named Edward Jenner was fascinated by this, and so he studied cowpox. He became convinced that, by injecting people with cowpox, he could protect them against the much worse disease smallpox. In 1796, he vaccinated a boy with cowpox and, two months later, with smallpox. The boy did not get smallpox. In the next two years, Jenner vaccinated several children in the same way, and none of them got the disease.

News of Jenner's success soon spread. In 1800, the Royal Vaccine Institution was founded in Berlin, Germany. In the following year, Napoleon opened a similar institute in Paris, France. It took nearly two centuries to achieve Jenner's dream of ridding the world of smallpox. In 1967, the World Health Organization (WHO) started an ambitious vaccination program, and the last known case of smallpox was recorded in Somalia in 1977.

The future of vaccinations aims at the eradication of three diseases that can be caused by mosquito bites: malaria, Zika virus, and dengue. Malaria is an infectious disease that is still a problem, in part because the virus that causes the disease hides in the cells away from the immune system. Zika virus has recently been discovered in various places all over the world, and it is particularly dangerous for pregnant women. At this time there is no vaccine for Zika virus, although scientists are working on one. Dengue is a disease that has multiplied alarmingly in recent years, but in the last two years a vaccine has been successfully developed for people between 9 and 45 years old.

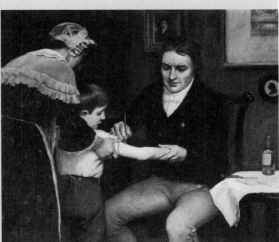

B Read the article about vaccinations. Complete the chart with the history of events in the story of vaccinations.

Date	Event
1. Early 16th century	Smallpox killed much of the native population in South America.
2. End of the 18th century	
3. 1796	
4. 1800	
5. 1801	
6. 1967	
7. 1977	
8. Future challenge	

5 Life in 2050

A Complete these predictions about life in 2050. Use the future continuous of the verb given. Then add two more predictions of your own.

Life on the moon?

By 2050, . . .

1. some people _____ will be living _____ in cities on the moon. (live)

2. many people _____ temperature-controlled body suits. (wear)

3. most people _____ cars that run on fuel from garbage. (drive)

4. people _____ in a new Olympic event – mind reading. (compete)

5. _____

   _____

6. _____

   _____

B Complete these predictions about what will have happened by 2050. Use the future perfect. Then add two more predictions of your own.

By 2050, . . .

1. computers _____ will have replaced _____ people as translators. (replace)

2. ties for men _____ out of fashion. (go)

3. scientists _____ a cheap way of getting drinking water from seawater. (discover)

4. medical researchers _____ a cure for cancer. (find)

5. _____

   _____

6. _____

   _____

A cure for cancer?

6 Write two responses to each question.

1. What will or won't you be doing in ten years? (Use the future continuous.)

   I won't be living with my parents.

   _____

2. How will cities of the future be different? (Use *will*.)

   Cities won't allow cars downtown.

   _____

3. How will life in small villages in your country have changed in the next 20 years?
   (Use the future perfect.)

   More people will have moved back from cities to small villages.

   _____

4. How do you think the world's weather will change during this century? (Use *will*.)

   The weather will be warmer, and the summers will be longer.

   _____

5. What advances will scientists have made by 2050? (Use the future perfect.)

   Scientists will have found a way to grow enough food for everyone.

   _____

7 Think of four more ways that technology will affect how we live and work in the next 20 years.

1. _Robots will be cleaning our homes._
2. _____
   _____
3. _____
   _____
4. _____
   _____
5. _____
   _____

8 Write two paragraphs about one of these topics or a topic of your choice. In the first paragraph, describe the past. In the second paragraph, describe how you think the future will be.

a music group	changes within a country	health
space exploration	changes within a region	technology

Eyeglasses were invented in the 13th century in Italy. These early glasses didn't include earpieces to keep the glasses on the wearer's face. Instead, they had to be held in front of the eyes or placed on the nose. In the 1700s, eyeglasses were designed with earpieces, making them easier to use. In the 20th century, contacts became common, making it even easier and more convenient for people to use corrective lenses.

Technological advances have continued to make vision correction more practical and convenient. In recent years, doctors have developed laser surgery techniques, which can make corrective lenses unnecessary for people with certain types of vision problems. In the future, computer technology will probably replace eyeglasses, contact lenses, and laser surgery. It may even make it possible for blind people to see.

_____
_____
_____
_____
_____
_____
_____
_____

11 Rites of passage

1 Milestones

A Read these statements. Check (✓) the ones that are true for you. For statements that are false, write the true information.

Example: As soon as I got my first cell phone, I called all my friends.

The moment I got a cell phone, I called my parents OR
I've never had a cell phone.

1. ☐ By the time I was three years old, I had already learned two languages.

_____

2. ☐ Before I started school, I was carefree – I used to watch TV all day.

_____

3. ☐ After I started taking the bus by myself, I became more independent.

_____

4. ☐ As soon as I got my driver's license, my parents let me drive everywhere.

_____

5. ☐ The moment I earned my own money, I opened a bank account.

_____

6. ☐ Once I started learning English, I quit studying other languages.

_____

7. ☐ Until I graduated from high school, I was very unsophisticated.

_____

8. ☐ Before I became more independent, I thought I knew more than my parents.

_____

B Write three true statements about how things have changed over time for you, your family, or your friends. Use time clauses.

1. _____

_____

2. _____

_____

3. _____

_____

2 Complete these descriptions. Use words from the box.

- ☐ ambitious
- ☐ argumentative
- ☐ carefree
- ☐ naive
- ☐ rebellious
- ☑ sophisticated

1. Sandra is so _____sophisticated_____. She always dresses well, she knows lots of intelligent people, and she never says anything silly.

2. I just spent a horrible evening with Patricia. She questioned and criticized everything I said. I wish she weren't so _____.

3. My sister is very _____. She trusts everyone and thinks everyone is good.

4. Once I turned 16, I became less _____, and my parents started to let me do what I wanted.

5. Eric is really _____. He wants to own his own business by the time he's 25.

6. I wish I could be like Susie. She's so _____ and never seems to worry about anything.

3 Do you have a friend who is special to you? Write about him or her. In the first paragraph, describe the person. In the second paragraph, describe a particular time when the person helped you.

One of my best friends is Jennifer. She's very mature and conscientious, and she always gives me good advice. Until I met her, I had been making some bad decisions . . . .

Jennifer is also very generous. She always helps her friends when they need it. For example, the moment she found out I was sick last winter, she came over and visited me.

_____

_____

_____

_____

_____

_____

_____

_____

A Scan the article from a sports magazine about Usain Bolt. What lesson did he learn as a child?

LEARNING FAST

Usain Bolt is called "Lightning" Bolt because he is considered the fastest man in the world. The Jamaican runner is an Olympic champion in the 100- and 200-meter **sprint**, as well as in the 4x100 relay, a race in which four runners each sprint 100 meters and then pass the baton to the next runner. He is the first man in the modern Olympic Games to win nine gold medals in the sprint. He is also the first athlete to win gold medals in the 100- and 200-meter races as well as in the 4x100 relay race in three Olympic Games, in 2008, 2012, and 2016.

In his autobiography, *Faster than Lightning*, Bolt writes that sports interested him most as a child. He also says that in school he learned something important about himself: he is ambitious because he loves to compete and to win.

He doesn't want to be one of the **runners-up**. This desire to be the best, plus his natural physical speed, brought him to the attention of Pablo McNeil, the former Olympic sprinter who was teaching athletics at Bolt's high school. Pablo McNeil convinced him to concentrate on sprinting and trained him in that sport.

When he was 15, Bolt **launched himself into** world-class athletics in the 2002 World Junior Championships in Jamaica's capital, Kingston. He was so nervous that he put his shoes on the wrong feet! But that was another important lesson: he would never allow stress to affect him again before a race. In spite of his nervousness, he became the youngest World Junior athlete to win the **prestigious** gold medal when he ran in the 200-meter sprint.

At the 2008 Olympic Games, Bolt learned another lesson: he should never stop learning. He broke two records at those games, becoming the fastest sprinter in the 100- and 200-meter race. At the end of the 100-meter race, he shocked everyone when he slowed down before the finish line. He was **ecstatic** because he already knew he was the winner. Some people felt he was too carefree. They thought he should have sprinted all the way. In the following 200-meter race, he didn't slow down. He ran all the way in **record time**, like the fastest man in the world.

B Read the article. Look at the words and phrases in bold in the article. Write definitions or synonyms for each word or phrase.

1. sprint _____

2. runners-up _____

3. launched himself into _____

4. prestigious _____

5. ecstatic _____

6. record time _____

C What factors mentioned in the article do you think have helped Usain Bolt to become a successful athlete?

_____

5 Write sentences about your regrets. Use *should (not) have.*

1. I spent all my money on clothes. Now I can't afford to take a vacation.

   I shouldn't have spent all my money on clothes.

2. I was very argumentative with my boss, so she fired me.

   _____

3. I changed jobs. Now I work in a bank. My job isn't very interesting.

   _____

4. I bought a new TV with my credit card. Now I can't afford the payments.

   _____

5. I studied music in school, but I'm much better at computer science.

   _____

6. I was completely rebellious when I was a student, so I got very bad grades.

   _____

7. My friend asked to copy my homework, so I let him. The teacher found out and gave us both Fs.

   _____

8. My cousin invited me to a party. I accepted but didn't put the
   date in my calendar. I forgot all about it.

   _____

9. I was very naive when I was younger. I lent money to people,
   but they hardly ever paid me back.

   _____

10. My friend asked for my opinion on her new hairstyle. I told her I didn't like it.
    Now she's not talking to me.

    _____

6 If . . .

A Rewrite the sentences as hypothetical situations. Use the words given.

1. I should have studied English sooner. (get a better job)

   If I'd studied English sooner, I would have gotten a better job.

2. We should have made a reservation. (eat already)

   _____

3. I should have put on sunscreen. (not get a sunburn)

   _____

4. You should have let me drive. (arrive by now)

   _____

5. I should have ignored your text in class. (not get in trouble)

   _____

B Write sentences describing hypothetical situations. Use the words given and your own ideas.

Can I borrow the car?

No, you haven't cleaned your room yet.

1. dependable _If I had been more dependable as a teenager,_

   my parents would have let me borrow the car more often.

2. ambitious _____

   _____

3. pragmatic _____

   _____

4. naive _____

   _____

5. rebellious _____

   _____

6. wise _____

   _____

7 **Complete the conversation. Circle the correct time expressions and use the correct tense of the verbs given.**

Hector: I've made such a mess of my life!

Scott: What do you mean?

Hector: If I ____hadn't accepted____
(not accept)

a job ((as soon as)/ before / until) I graduated,

I _____ around
(travel)

South America all summer – just like you did.

You were so carefree.

Scott: You know, I should _____
(not go)

to South America.

I should _____
(take)

the great job I was offered. (After / Before /

Until) I returned from South America,

it was too late.

Hector: But my job is so depressing! (Before / The moment / Until) I started it,

I hated it – on the very first day! That was five years ago, and nothing's changed.

I should _____ for another job right away.
(look)

Scott: Well, start looking now. I posted my résumé online last month, and five companies contacted

me right away. If I _____ my résumé, no one _____ me.
(not post)   (contact)

I accepted one of the job offers.

Hector: Really? What's the job?

Scott: It's working as a landscape gardener. (Before / The moment / Until)

I saw it, I knew it was right for me.

Hector: But for me right now, the problem is that I get a very good salary and I just bought a house.

If I _____ the house, I _____ take a lower paying job.
(not buy)   (be able to)

Scott: Well, I guess you can't have everything. If I _____ a better salary,
(have)

I _____ a house, too.
(buy)

12 Keys to success

1 Complete these sentences with *In order for* or *In order to.*

1. <u>In order for</u> a restaurant to be popular, it has to have attractive decor.

2. _____ a movie to be entertaining, it has to have good actors and an interesting story.

3. _____ succeed in business, you often have to work long hours.

4. _____ attract new members, a sports club needs to offer inexpensive memberships.

5. _____ speak a foreign language well, it's a good idea to use the language as often as possible.

6. _____ a clothing store to succeed, it has to be able to find the latest fashions.

2 Write sentences. Use the information in the box.

☐ have talented salespeople	☐ work extremely long hours
☑ keep up with your studies	☐ provide excellent customer service
☐ be clever and entertaining	☐ have drama and interesting characters

1. be a successful student

   <u>In order to be a successful student, you have to keep up with your studies.</u>

2. a clothes store to be profitable

   <u>For a clothes store to be profitable,</u> _____

3. manage your own business

   _____

4. an advertisement to be persuasive

   _____

5. run a successful automobile company

   _____

6. a reality TV show to be successful

   _____

3 Choose the correct word or phrase.

1. I didn't enjoy this book on how to succeed in business. It wasn't very
   <u>   well written   </u>. (affordable / well paid / **well written**)

2. I learned a lot about how to run a successful bookstore from taking that class.
   I found it very _____. (attractive / informative / knowledgeable)

3. Annie has so many interesting ideas, and she's always thinking of new projects.
   She's very _____. (clever / entertaining / tough)

4. Debra is a salesperson, and she's good at her job. She's so _____
   that she sells three times as much as her co-workers. (unfriendly / affordable / persuasive)

5. Matthew is one of the top models in Milan. He goes to the gym every day,
   so he looks really _____. (clever / charming / muscular)

6. Before opening a new store, it's important to think through all of your ideas and have
   _____. (competitive salaries / a clear business plan / a reliable job)

7. My new job has great benefits. We have unlimited time off, excellent health insurance, and
   _____. (a good product / flexible working hours / a crowdfunding platform)

4 Read this information about journalists. Then write a paragraph about one of the people in the box or another person of your choice.

To be a successful journalist, you need to be both talented and dynamic. You have to write well and write quickly. In order to report the news, a journalist needs to have a good knowledge of world and current events. In addition, you must be able to report a story accurately.

| an artist | a boss | a homemaker | a parent | a teacher |

_____
_____
_____
_____
_____
_____
_____
_____

5 | I like it because . . .

A For each pair of pictures, write one sentence about what you like and one sentence about what you dislike. Give reasons using the words given.

1. <u>I like this park because it's clean</u>   <u>I don't like this park since</u>
<u>and there are a lot of trees.</u> (because)   _____ (since)

2. _____   _____
_____ (since)   _____ (the reason)

3. _____   _____
_____ (because of)   _____ (due to)

B Think of an example in your city of each of these places: a restaurant, a hotel, and a shopping center. Write a sentence about why you like or dislike each one.

Example: <u>The reason I don't like Cho Dang Gol Restaurant in my hometown is its noisy location</u>
<u>right by the freeway.</u>

1. _____

2. _____

3. _____

6 A new business with an ancient product

A Scan the article about Andean Grain. What is the secret that the company is selling?

SELLING SECRETS OF THE PAST

The Argentinian company Andean Grain is contributing to a **comeback** of highly nutritious foods that were unknown to many people during the last few hundred years. Andean Grain sells foods made from **indigenous** Latin American plants, like chia seeds, amaranth, and quinoa. These plants are coming **to prominence** today because knowledgeable people have discovered that chia seeds, amaranth, and quinoa are **superfoods**, incredibly rich in vitamins and proteins.

Chia seeds were grown by the Aztecs as an energy food. In order to travel long distances without having to stop, they drank a beverage consisting of chia seeds, lemon juice, and water. The Aztecs also cultivated amaranth, which they believed was a superfood, as do scientists today. Quinoa was grown in the mountains of the Andes by the Incas. All three of these foods **went out of favor** after the conquest of Latin America in the 16th century. Wheat was preferred over these native plants, and they were almost unknown outside the countries that grew them. Nevertheless, these foods have become popular once more due to the health benefits that they are supposed to provide.

They appear to be of optimal benefit for the heart and brain, and **rumor has it** that they may help prevent cancer. They're also gluten-free. Because many people today have problems digesting the gluten in wheat, gluten-free foods have become very fashionable.

As a result, there is a great demand by the public for these superfoods. Andean Grain sells its products all over the world, but it is especially active in Europe, where it has a main office in the United Kingdom. From its base in Argentina, Andean Grain sends most of its native plants to Europe to be made into affordable breads, breakfast cereals, and today's popular trail mixes, which are combinations of dried fruits, nuts, and seeds.

The secret is out, and what was hidden from the world for so many centuries has today become an important discovery of foods for our health. Did you know about these superfoods before the rest of the world discovered them just a few years ago?

B Read the article. Look at the words and phrases in bold in the article. Write definitions or synonyms for each word or phrase.

1. comeback _____

2. indigenous _____

3. to prominence _____

4. superfood _____

5. went out of favor _____

6. rumor has it _____

7 Look at these advertisements and write two sentences about each one. Describe the features and give reasons why you like or dislike the advertisements.

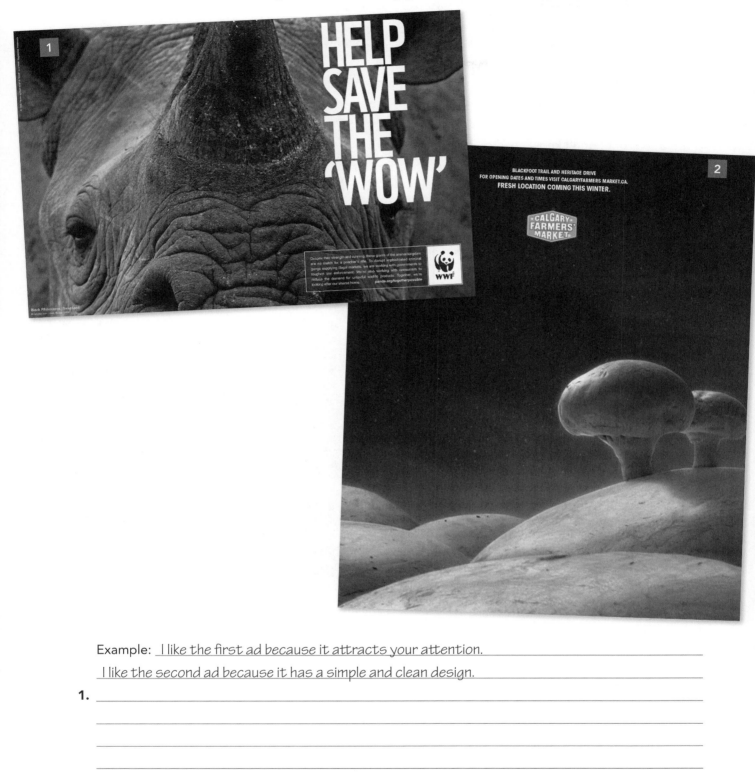

Example: I like the first ad because it attracts your attention.

I like the second ad because it has a simple and clean design.

1. _____

_____

_____

_____

2. _____

_____

_____

_____

8 Do you have the right qualities?

A Complete the sentences with the words from the box.

affordable	athletic	clever	entertaining	informative	knowledgeable	muscular	salesperson

1. I'm not _____ enough about tools to be a successful salesperson in a hardware store. I'm familiar with some common tools, but I don't know how to use most tools.

2. To be successful, personal trainers need to be fit and _____.

3. *Weekend Talk* ran for only three months because it was so boring. For a TV show to be successful on Saturday evenings, it really has to be _____.

4. I wouldn't be a good _____ because I'm not very persuasive.

5. I found a fantastic news website this morning. It's really _____. It has very detailed stories about local and international news.

6. For a salesperson to be persuasive, he or she has to be _____ with words.

7. Kate is so _____. She plays soccer, tennis, and basketball, and she's excellent at all three sports.

8. I like this store, but it's not very _____. Even the small items are expensive.

B Write sentences using the words below and infinitive clauses with *to* or *for*.

1. apply for a job / write a good résumé

   _____

2. be an effective personal trainer / listen to your clients' needs

   _____

3. a restaurant / be successful / delicious food at good prices

   _____

4. students / get good grades / study hard and do their best

   _____

5. learn a new language / practice every day

   _____

1 **What do you think happened? Write an explanation for each event using past modals.**

1. _She may have lost her car key._

2. _____

3. _____

4. _____

5. _____

6. _____

2 Write two paragraphs about something strange that has happened to you. In the first paragraph, describe the situation. In the second paragraph, give two or three explanations for what happened.

> I invited six friends to a barbecue on the beach. I suggested we meet at eight o'clock. They all said they would come and bring some food.
>
> On the day of the barbecue, only two of my friends showed up. I guess my other friends could have overslept, or they might have decided to do something else. Another possibility is that they may have thought I meant 8 P.M. instead of 8 A.M. I'm not sure what happened!

_____
_____
_____
_____
_____
_____
_____
_____

3 Answer these questions. Write two explanations using past modals.

Why do you think the ancient Britons built Stonehenge?

1. They might have _built it to use as a church._ _____

2. _____
_____

3. They could have _____
_____

4. _____
_____

How do you think early explorers communicated with people in the places they visited?

5. They may have _____
_____

6. _____
_____

How do you think the early Polynesians were able to travel across vast oceans?

4 Strange creatures

A Skim the online article about a world-famous legend. Where does the legend come from?

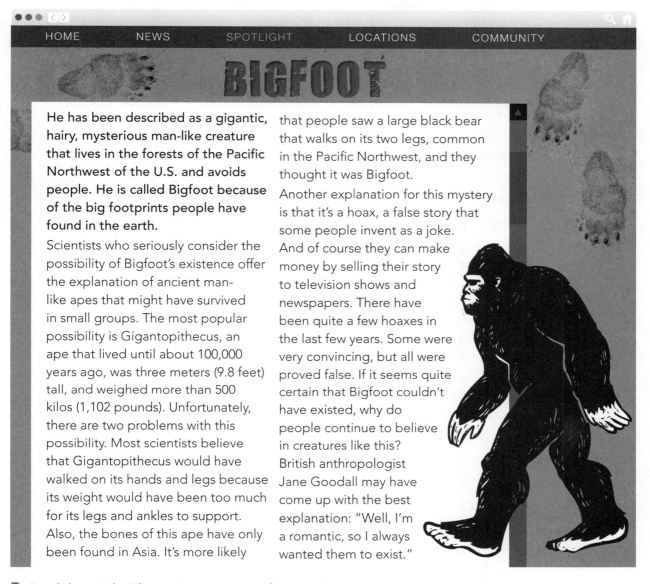

HOME   NEWS   SPOTLIGHT   LOCATIONS   COMMUNITY

BIGFOOT

He has been described as a gigantic, hairy, mysterious man-like creature that lives in the forests of the Pacific Northwest of the U.S. and avoids people. He is called Bigfoot because of the big footprints people have found in the earth.

Scientists who seriously consider the possibility of Bigfoot's existence offer the explanation of ancient man-like apes that might have survived in small groups. The most popular possibility is Gigantopithecus, an ape that lived until about 100,000 years ago, was three meters (9.8 feet) tall, and weighed more than 500 kilos (1,102 pounds). Unfortunately, there are two problems with this possibility. Most scientists believe that Gigantopithecus would have walked on its hands and legs because its weight would have been too much for its legs and ankles to support. Also, the bones of this ape have only been found in Asia. It's more likely that people saw a large black bear that walks on its two legs, common in the Pacific Northwest, and they thought it was Bigfoot.

Another explanation for this mystery is that it's a hoax, a false story that some people invent as a joke. And of course they can make money by selling their story to television shows and newspapers. There have been quite a few hoaxes in the last few years. Some were very convincing, but all were proved false. If it seems quite certain that Bigfoot couldn't have existed, why do people continue to believe in creatures like this? British anthropologist Jane Goodall may have come up with the best explanation: "Well, I'm a romantic, so I always wanted them to exist."

B Read the article. Then write answers to the questions.

1. How might someone describe Bigfoot?

   _____

2. Imagine that you have seen a creature resembling Bigfoot. Do you think you would have believed it was Bigfoot? Why or why not?

   _____

3. What is the most popular possible explanation for Bigfoot from scientists?

   _____

4. What is one problem with this popular explanation?

   _____

5. What do you think people might have seen when they thought they saw Bigfoot?

   _____

5 Should have, could have, would have

A What should or shouldn't these people have done? Read each situation and check (✓) the best suggestion.

1. Mrs. King wouldn't let her children watch TV for a month because they broke a window playing baseball.

   ☐ She could have made them pay for the window.

   ☐ She shouldn't have done anything. It was an accident.

   ☐ She shouldn't have let them play baseball for a month.

2. Steve's old car broke down on the highway late one night, and his cell phone battery was dead. He left the car on the side of the road and walked home.

   ☐ He should have stopped a stranger's car to ask for a ride.

   ☐ He could have slept in his car till morning.

   ☐ He should have walked to the nearest pay phone and called a tow truck.

3. Sarah was in a park. She saw some people leave all their trash after they had finished their picnic. She did nothing.

   ☐ She did the right thing.

   ☐ She should have asked them to throw away their trash.

   ☐ She could have thrown away the trash herself.

4. Edward's neighbors were renovating their kitchen. They made a lot of noise every day until midnight. Edward called the police.

   ☐ He shouldn't have called the police.

   ☐ He should have realized that they were trying to finish the job quickly.

   ☐ He could have asked them not to make any noise in the evenings.

5. Barbara's boss borrowed $20 from her a month ago, but he forgot to pay her back. Barbara never said anything about it.

   ☐ She should have demanded her money back.

   ☐ She shouldn't have loaned it to him.

   ☐ She could have written him a nice email asking for the money.

B What would you have done in the situations in part A? Write suggestions or comments using past modals.

1. _I would have made them pay for the window._

2. _____

3. _____

4. _____

5. _____

6 Nouns and verbs

A Complete the chart.

Noun	Verb	Noun	Verb
assumption	_assume_	_____	predict
criticism	_____	suggestion	_____
demand	_____	suspect	_____
excuse	_____	warning	_____

B Complete the sentences using words from the chart in part A. For the verbs, use *shouldn't have* + past participle. For the nouns, use the appropriate singular or plural form.

1. Last year some economists said that food and gas prices wouldn't increase. Those _____predictions_____ were wrong! Both food and gas are more expensive now.

2. Christopher _____ having a beach party. It was so dark, I stepped in a hole and hurt my ankle.

3. Andy bought an expensive ring and gave it to Millie for her birthday. A year later, he asked her to marry him. When she said no, he made an outrageous _____. He said he wanted his ring back!

4. I _____ my co-worker not to be late for work so often. It was really none of my business.

5. Lori said she was late because she got caught in traffic. Hmm. I've heard that _____ before.

6. Kevin _____ I would still be awake at midnight. I was asleep when he called.

7. I thought that my roommate had taken my wallet, but I found it at the bottom of my bag. I _____ that my roommate took it. He would never do something like that.

8. James _____ me for wearing jeans and a T-shirt to a friend's party. He always has negative things to say.

7 Complete these conversations. Use the past modals in the box and the verbs given. (More than one modal is possible.)

could have	may have	might have	must have	should have

1. **A:** Where's Luke? He's late.

   B: He _____may have gotten_____ (get) stuck in rush-hour traffic.

   A: He's always late! You know, he _____should have taken_____ (take) the subway.

2. **A:** Judy never responded to my invitation.

   B: She _____ (not receive) it. You _____ (call) her.

3. **A:** Matt hasn't answered his phone for a week.

   B: He _____ (go) on vacation. He _____ (tell) you, though – sometimes he's very inconsiderate.

4. **A:** I can never get in touch with Kathy. She never returns phone calls or answers texts!

   B: Yeah, I have the same problem with her. Her voice mail _____ (run out) of space. She _____ (get) a new phone service by now.

5. **A:** Thomas is strange. Sometimes he works really hard, but sometimes he seems pretty lazy. Last week, he hardly did any work.

   B: Well, you know, he _____ (not feel) well. Still, he _____ (tell) you that he was sick.

6. **A:** I ordered a book online a month ago, but it still hasn't arrived.

   B: They _____ (have) a problem with the warehouse, but they _____ (let) you know.

14 Creative careers

1 Complete the conversation. Use the passive form of the verbs given.

Anna: Putting on a fashion show must be really fun!

Marcus: Yeah, but it's also challenging. All the clothes have to _____be numbered_____ (number) so that the models wear them in the right sequence. And they also have to _____ (mark) with the name of the right model.

Anna: What happens if something _____ (wear) by the wrong model?

Marcus: Well, if it doesn't fit, it looks terrible! First impressions are very important. A lot of clothes _____ (sell) because they look good at the show.

Anna: Do you have to rehearse for a fashion show?

Marcus: Of course! There's more involved than just models and clothes. Special lighting _____ (use), and music _____ (play) during the show.

Anna: It sounds complicated.

Marcus: Oh, it is. And at some fashion shows, a commentary may _____ (give).

Anna: A commentary? What do you mean?

Marcus: Well, someone talks about the clothes as they _____ (show) on the runway by the models.

Anna: It sounds like timing is really important.

Marcus: Exactly. Everything has to _____ (time) perfectly! Otherwise, the show may _____ (ruin).

2 Choose the correct words or phrases.

1. Often, special music has to be _____ for a film.
(written / designed / hired)

2. A play may be _____ for several weeks before it is shown to the public.
(shot / taken / rehearsed)

3. Designing _____ for actors to wear requires a lot of creativity.
(scripts / movies / clothes)

4. Newspapers are _____ to stores after they are printed.
(written / delivered / reported)

5. _____ are added after the film has been put together.
(Scenes / Sound effects / Actors)

3 Complete this passage. Use the passive form of the verbs given.

1. Nowadays, all sorts of things _____<u>are produced</u>_____ (produce) in factories, including lettuce!
At one food factory, fresh green lettuce _____ (grow) without sunlight or soil.
Here is how it _____ (do).

2. Lettuce seedlings _____ (place) at one end of a long production line.
Conveyor belts _____ (use) to move the seedlings slowly along. The tiny plants
_____ (expose) to light from fluorescent lamps.

3. They have to _____ (feed) through the roots with plant food and water that
_____ (control) by a computer.

4. Thirty days later, the plants _____ (collect) at the other end of the conveyor belts.

5. They may _____ (deliver) to the vegetable market the same day.

A Scan the article and use the past participle form of the words in the box to complete the sentences with the passive voice.

concern   create   inspire   interest   interview   notice

A Passion for Fashion

In just the last ten years, a new job category has been [1]_____: professional fashion blogger. The story of one of the very first professional bloggers is an inspiration to young people everywhere who are [2]_____ with how to make a good living while also doing something that is important to them.

In 2007, Imran Amed, a young Canadian-British citizen who had recently moved to London, decided to take advantage of some free time he had while he wasn't busy working at his job. He sat down in his living room and began to write about something he was passionately [3]_____ in: fashion. Sitting on his sofa, he created a blog that allowed him to communicate with readers who shared his fascination with the fashion industry. Naturally, at the beginning, his readers were mainly his friends and family. But because of his ability to tell interesting and perceptive stories that made readers want to keep on reading, his blog was soon [4]_____ by many people, and by professionals in the industry.

In time, advertisers began to pay Amed's blog, *The Business of Fashion*, for the opportunity to connect with all those readers and potential clients. Amed was also an excellent interviewer. His interviews with Karl Lagerfeld, Natalie Massenet, Nick Knight, and other giants in the fashion industry became another great attraction to his blog. Designers were willing to be [5]_____ by him because his questions and comments were relevant, intelligent, and [6]_____ by his passion for fashion.

Today, professionals in 200 countries consider *The Business of Fashion*

Imran Amed, accepting the Business of Fashion Media Award at the 2016 CFDA Fashion Awards

to be required reading in order to keep up with the latest developments in fashion. Thirty employees now fill the demand for information on fashion. More recent fashion blogs like Chiara Ferragni's *The Blonde Salad* in Italy and Sabina Hernandez's blog *Te lo dije nena (I told you, girl)* in Argentina are now also very successful.

Potential professional bloggers, take note: passionate interest is fundamental to success. If you can discover your passion, then the power of that energy will be the magnet that captures and holds your readers' attention. That is exactly what happened one day when Imran Amed sat down and began to write a blog on his sofa.

B Read the article. Check (✓) the true statements according to the article. For the statements that are false, write the true information.

1. ☐ Imran Amed has always lived in London.

_____

2. ☐ His family and friends are not interested in fashion and do not read about it.

_____

3. ☐ Because Imran Amed knows how to tell an interesting story, many people began to read his blog.

_____

4. ☐ Designers enjoy giving interviews to Imran Amed because his questions are intelligent and show that he is interested in fashion.

_____

5. ☐ Chiara Ferragni's and Sabina Hernandez's blogs were started before *The Business of Fashion*.

_____

6. ☐ If you want to be a professional blogger, the most important thing you will need for success is money.

_____

5 **Join these sentences with *who* or *that*. Add a comma wherever one is needed.**

broadcast presenter

junior newspaper reporter

Examples:

Broadcast presenters are journalists.

They report the news on television.

Broadcast presenters are journalists who report the news on television.

A junior newspaper reporter should be curious.

He or she is often new to journalism.

A junior newspaper reporter, who is often new to journalism, should be curious.

1. An editorial director chooses only the most interesting stories.

He or she tells the reporters what news stories to cover.

_____

_____

2. A game animator is a skilled artist.

He or she creates detailed graphics for computer games.

_____

_____

3. A storyboard artist is a creative person.

He or she illustrates plans for individual scenes for a movie.

_____

_____

4. Stunt people perform dangerous moves in films and TV shows.

The films and shows have a lot of action scenes.

_____

_____

5. TV sitcoms include actors and actresses.

They are recognized by television viewers around the world.

_____

_____

6 Match the definitions with the jobs.

1. a cinematographer __g__
2. a film editor _____
3. a gossip columnist _____
4. a graphic designer _____
5. a club DJ _____
6. a band manager _____
7. a web content manager _____
8. a talk show host _____

a. a journalist who specializes in reporting on the personal lives of famous people

b. someone who plays music in a dance club

c. someone that helps a movie director put together the best "takes"

d. a person who is in charge of choosing the text and pictures on a website

e. a TV personality who invites guests to come on his or her program

f. a person who takes care of business for a band

g. a person who operates the main camera during shooting

h. someone that creates the design for a printed work

7 Choose a job from Exercise 6 or another job you're interested in. In the first paragraph, describe the job. In the second paragraph, explain why the job interests you. Use relative clauses in some of your descriptions.

I'd like to be a band manager for a rock or pop band. Band managers are the people who schedule concerts and shows for bands. They also help bands make creative decisions about things like CD covers, magazine interviews, and even music. In addition, band managers who know people in the music business can help a band become successful.

This job interests me because I love music, and I enjoy being around people who sing and play instruments. Also, I'm organized and reliable, and I think that I have the skills that a good band manager needs.

_____
_____
_____
_____
_____

8 Describe six steps in the process of renovating a restaurant. Use the passive form of the verbs given below.

designer

builders

painters

electrician

delivery people

reopening

1. First, <u>a renovation plan is approved.</u> (a renovation plan / approve)

2. Next, _____ (new walls / build)

3. Then _____ (the walls / paint)

4. After that, _____ (new lighting / install)

5. Then _____ (new furniture / deliver)

6. Finally, _____ (the restaurant / reopen)

15 A law must be passed!

1 **What should be done about each situation? Write sentences about these pictures, giving your opinion. Use the passive form with *should*, *shouldn't*, or *ought to*.**

Leaving large items on the sidewalk

Eating on the subway

Playing loud music in your apartment

Letting dogs run without leashes

1. _People shouldn't be allowed to leave large items on the sidewalk._   OR
   People ought to be required to take large items to designated dumps.

2. _____

   _____

3. _____

   _____

4. _____

   _____

2 **Make recommendations about the situations in these pictures.
Use the passive form with *has to, has got to, must,* or *mustn't*.**

1. <u>A law has to be passed to prevent people from losing their homes.</u>   OR
   <u>Something must be done to repair abandoned homes.</u>

2. _____
   _____

3. _____

4. _____
   _____

3 Think of four things that you have strong opinions about. Write your opinions and explain your reasons for them. Use passive modals.

Example: _In my opinion, cell phones shouldn't be allowed in class._
They distract students from the lesson.

1. I feel that _____

_____

2. I think that _____

_____

3. In my opinion, _____

_____

4. I don't think that _____

_____

4 Respond to these opinions by giving a different one of your own. Use expressions from the box.

> That's interesting, but I think . . .
> That's not a bad idea. On the other hand, I feel . . .
> You may have a point. However, I think . . .
> Do you? I'm not sure . . .

1. A: Everyone should be required to
study Chinese.

B: _You may have a point. However, I think_
that English is more useful for traveling.

2. A: People mustn't be allowed to write unkind
things about others on social networking sites.

B: _____

_____

3. A: Public transportation should be provided free
of charge.

B: _____

_____

4. A: I think people ought to be required to buy
hybrid cars.

B: _____

_____

5. A: In my opinion, all plastic containers should
be banned.

B: _____

_____

5 **Getting revenge**

A Skim the web posts. What is a revenge story? Why is each of these stories a revenge story?

DO YOU HAVE A REVENGE STORY? SHARE IT!

1. Marcy: I used to have a friend who was a lot of fun. She always loved to go out to eat. There was just one small problem: Every time the server brought the check, she would say, "Uh-oh! I don't have enough money with me. Can I pay you back later?" This was OK the first and second time it happened, but these excuses happened again and again. I finally got my revenge. The next time we went out for dinner, I said that I had forgotten my wallet. She was shocked, but she paid the check. However, she has never called me to go out again. I guess she was a moocher – a person who always tries to get someone else to pay.

2. Jonathan: My neighbors used to keep rabbits in their yard, but they treated them very badly. Rabbit pens should be cleaned regularly, but these rabbits were dirty, and the smell was really terrible. Worse, I noticed that the rabbits didn't have enough to eat or drink. When I complained to my neighbors, they said, "It's not your problem." When I called the animal protection society, they said they would investigate. I waited a week, but nothing happened. One night, I stole the rabbits and took them home. The next day I gave them to a local pet store.

3. Chad: I was having problems sleeping because of a dripping noise coming from my air conditioner. I thought the air conditioner needed to be repaired, so I called a technician. She couldn't find anything wrong with it, but she said the dripping was coming from the apartment above me. I asked my neighbor to have his air conditioner checked, but he said, "If you can't sleep, that's your problem!" The following day I climbed a ladder and turned off the electricity inside the air conditioner. My neighbor had to call the technician to turn it on, and when she did, she also fixed the dripping. It cost him a few dollars, but it was worth it!

B Read the comments. Do you agree or disagree? Write *A* (agree) or *D* (disagree).

_____ **1.** Marcy shouldn't have pretended to lose her wallet. She should have spoken with her friend and told her it was time she paid for a meal.

_____ **2.** I think Marcy did exactly what she ought to have done. Moochers must be taught a lesson!

_____ **3.** People mustn't be permitted to steal. Jonathan made a big mistake, didn't he?

_____ **4.** If people don't take care of their animals, something has got to be done. However, I don't think he should have stolen the rabbits.

_____ **5.** Sometimes neighbors must be taught a lesson. Chad didn't hurt anybody, so I think his nasty neighbor got what he deserved.

_____ **6.** You may have a point about some neighbors, but I think Chad should have called the manager of his building.

C Do you think getting revenge – doing something mean to someone in return – is acceptable behavior? Why or why not?

_____

_____

_____

6 Add tag questions to these statements.

1. Bullying is a serious problem, _____ isn't it _____?
2. The city doesn't provide enough services for elderly people, _____ does it _____?
3. You can easily spend all your money on food and rent, _____?
4. Some unemployed people don't really want to work, _____?
5. Health care is getting more and more expensive, _____?
6. There are a lot of homeless people downtown, _____?
7. Some schools have overcrowded classrooms, _____?
8. Laws should be passed to reduce street crime, _____?

7 Nouns and verbs

A Complete the chart.

Noun	Verb	Noun	Verb
advertisement	_advertise_	_____	pollute
_____	bully	prohibition	_____
_____	improve	provision	_____
offense	_____	_____	require
permission	_____	_____	vandalize

B Write sentences with tag questions using words from the chart. Use four of the nouns and four of the verbs.

1. _Bicyclists should be required to wear helmets,_
   shouldn't they?

2. _____

3. _____

4. _____

5. _____

6. _____

7. _____

8. _____

9. _____

8 Give one reason for and one reason against these opinions.

1. Children should be made to study a foreign language in primary school.

For: *It would help children understand other cultures.*

Against: *I don't think it would be easy to find enough teachers.*

2. Schools should punish students who bully other children.

For: _____

Against: _____

3. More tax money ought to be spent on cleaning up vandalism.

For: _____

Against: _____

4. Stray animals should be cared for in animal shelters.

For: _____

Against: _____

9 Complete the conversation. Use passive modals and tag questions.

Gina: You know, I just moved into this new apartment building, and I thought everything would be really great now.

Alec: What's the problem?

Gina: Well, yesterday, the manager gave me a copy of the house rules. I found out that I can't park my moped on the sidewalk in front of the building anymore.

Alec: But people shouldn't _____ (permit) to park their bikes or mopeds there.

Gina: Why not? There isn't any other place to park, _____? I guess I'll have to park on the street now.

Alec: I'm sorry that parking somewhere else will be inconvenient, but don't you agree that people shouldn't _____ (allow) to block the sidewalk or the entrance to the building?

Gina: Well, you may have a point, but parking spaces for all types of cycles need _____ (provide) for renters here. All renters with a car have a parking space, _____?

Alec: Well, yes, you're right. You should go to the next renters' meeting and discuss the issue with everyone else.

Gina: That's not a bad idea. My voice ought _____ (hear) as much as anyone else's – I think I will!

16 Reaching your goals

1 Match each profession with the correct achievement.

☐ actor   ☐ student   ☐ volunteer
☐ parent   ☐ nurse   ☑ high school counselor

1. I've managed to help hundreds of students get into college. _high school counselor_
2. I was able to clean litter from dozens of beaches over the last three years. _____
3. I managed to maintain an A average during my last four years of school. _____
4. I've been able to work with many of my favorite movie stars. _____
5. I've managed to teach my children how to be responsible citizens. _____
6. I've been able to help sick people feel better. _____

2 Choosing a job

A Complete the chart with your own ideas.

Job	Goals of people with this profession	
1. social worker	_help people_	_____
2. university professor	_educate people_	_____
3. small-business owner	_____	_____
4. emergency-room nurse	_____	_____

B Complete these sentences with your ideas from part A. Try to add more details.

1. As a social worker, Jane hopes she'll _have helped poor and elderly people in her community._
   She'd also like to have _____
2. As a university professor three years from now, Paul hopes he'll have _____
   _____
   He'd also like to have _____
   _____
3. By this time next year, Jake, a small business owner, would like to have _____
   _____
   In addition, he hopes he'll have _____
   _____
4. In the next five years, Amy, an emergency-room nurse, hopes she'll have _____
   _____
   In addition, she'd like to have _____

3 **Write two paragraphs about an issue that is important to you. In the first paragraph, describe a past achievement related to that issue. In the second paragraph, describe a goal.**

Last year, I began volunteering at a local animal shelter. I managed to help find homes for over twenty cats and dogs in one year. It was an incredibly rewarding experience.

In the next few years, I hope to help more animals find homes. I'd like to have placed a hundred pets in homes over the next four years.

A Scan the first paragraph of the article. Where is Rupert Isaacson from? Where are his parents from? Where did he go?

RUPERT ISAACSON

Rupert Isaacson is a man who has faced a major challenge in his life. The son of parents who were born in Africa, he grew up in London and in the English countryside, where he discovered his love of horses. Because he grew up hearing so many fascinating memories about Africa from his parents, he went there and lived with nomadic people called the Bushmen of the Kalahari Desert. He then wrote a book, *The Healing Land*, about his experiences with the Bushmen and the problems of survival they face in the twenty-first century.

By the year 2000, Rupert was already managing to make a living as a journalist, writing articles and guidebooks about Africa and India. It was in India that he met his wife, Kristin. Today, they live with their son, Rowan, just outside of Austin, Texas, in the U.S. But Rupert faced the greatest challenge of his life when, at the age of two, Rowan was diagnosed with autism, a condition that affects people's ability to communicate and interact socially with others.

Rupert discovered that spending time with horses and riding them was helping Rowan. The presence of the horses was very calming to the boy. Rupert also knew that the Bushmen of the Kalahari possessed great knowledge about healing. He thought that if he could find a group of people with healing powers and a great knowledge of horses, there could be a possibility of helping his son. Unfortunately, the Bushmen of the Kalahari do not have horses.

So the family set off for Mongolia, where horses have been important for thousands of years. Rupert has written about this journey dedicated to helping his son in *Horse Boy*, and he has produced a documentary of the same name. In the film, viewers have the opportunity to see the family traveling in Mongolia, riding horses, and meeting healers in order to help Rowan.

Because working with horses has helped Rowan, Rupert established The Horse Boy Foundation at his ranch in Texas. It is a school that teaches people how to use horses for healing. In addition to writing another book, *The Long Ride Home*, about traveling with Rowan to Africa, Australia, and Arizona in the U.S., Rupert has also produced the documentary *Endangerous*, with Rowan as host, about dangerous animals that are threatened with extinction. Rupert Isaacson has managed to discover the secret of turning one challenge into many accomplishments.

B Read the article. What is the challenge that Rupert Isaacson faced? What was one of the solutions to this challenge that Rupert found?

Challenge: _____

Solution: _____

C Answer the questions.

1. How does autism affect people?

_____

2. Why did Rupert's family go to Mongolia?

_____

3. What is the purpose of The Horse Boy Foundation?

_____

4. What does Rowan do in *Endangerous*?

_____

5. List three accomplishments of Rupert Isaacson.

_____

5 Choose the correct word.

1. It's not good to be _____
if you're an emergency-room nurse.
(courageous / timid / upbeat)

2. If teachers are going to be successful, they
have to be _____.
(dependent / rigid / resourceful)

3. You have to be _____
if you work as a volunteer.
(adaptable / cynical / unimaginative)

4. If you take a job far from your family and friends,
you have to be _____.
(compassionate / dependent / self-sufficient)

5. One of the most important things about
working with children is being positive
and not _____.
(adaptable / cynical / resourceful)

6. Being a role model for troubled youths
requires someone who is strong and

_____.

(compassionate / insensitive / timid)

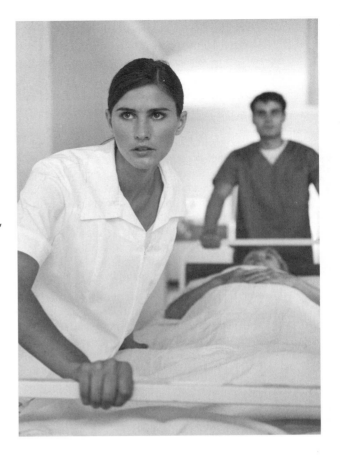

6 Read each sentence. Write A for achievement or G for goal.

1. I've been able to provide clean water to
three villages during my time as a Peace
Corps volunteer. _____

2. By the time I'm 35, I'd like to have lived
in a culture that's very different from
my own. _____

3. While I was working abroad in
Tokyo, I managed to learn to speak
Japanese fluently. _____

4. After my time with Habitat for Humanity,
I hope to have made a significant and
positive difference in people's lives. _____

5. I'd like to have gotten another degree in
two years. _____

6. I hope I'll have gotten married by the
time I'm 30. _____

7 Accomplishments and goals

A Match the verbs with the nouns. Write the collocations. (More than one answer may be possible.)

Verb	Noun
buy	a change
get	debts
learn	a house
make	a promotion
meet	new skills
pay off	someone special

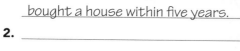

1. <u>   buy a house   </u>
2. _____
3. _____
4. _____
5. _____
6. _____

B Write one sentence about an accomplishment and another sentence about a goal. Use the words in part A and your own ideas.

1. <u>My sister and her husband have managed to save enough money to buy a house. I expect to have bought a house within five years.</u>

2. _____
_____
_____

3. _____
_____
_____
_____

4. _____
_____
_____
_____

5. _____
_____
_____

6. _____
_____
_____
_____

Personal portraits

A Write three sentences about the accomplishments of someone you know very well. Use the present perfect or simple past.

By investing his money carefully, my neighbor Enrico was able to retire at 40. Since then, he has managed to set up an organization that helps find jobs for people who are homeless. In addition, he has volunteered his time at a homeless shelter in the city.

_____

_____

_____

_____

B Write three sentences about things the same person would like to have achieved in ten years. Use the future perfect or *would like to have* + past participle.

Enrico would like to have started an organization to provide scholarships for needy college students by the time he's 50. He hopes to travel a lot, too. In fact, he hopes he'll have traveled all through Southeast Asia.

_____

_____

_____

_____